Rooted
fifty-two weeks of intention

Printed in the United States of America

Kindle Direct Publishing

Cover Art: Purely Drea | www.purelydrea.com

A note from the author:

This guided journal was created for you to self-explore and self-express. Journaling has always been an outlet for my emotions when facing challenges and celebrating joys throughout my life. Many of the prompts in this book have encouraged me to lean in and surface some of my deepest thoughts. I was able to find immense healing through the intentions and affirmations God placed on my heart.

My hope is that no matter where you start, these prompts will be on time for whatever you are facing or releasing this season.

I have prayed over this book, over you, and over your growth from start to finish. May you seek and find the peace that surpasses all understanding as you continue to dive deeper into living intentionally.

always love,
ka'ala

For my mother who loves selflessly.
For my father – one day at a time.

For anyone who could use these reminders:
You are strong enough for this.
Water yourself.
Celebrate your bloom.

Rooted
fifty-two weeks of intention
a guided journal
by ka'ala

table of contents

week one

intentional living

...in my goals, my work, my words, and my actions.
I will have thought and meaning behind what I do.

What are my immediate goals?

_____

_____

_____

_____

Three things I will intentionally cut back on this week:

_____

_____

_____

_____

Three constructive things I will intentionally add to my life this week:

_____

_____

_____

_____

Intention:

_____

Affirmation:

_____

I am grateful for:

_____

_____

_____

_____

Personal Prayer/ Meditation/ Journal Entry:

week two

patience

I will not rush the process - be it work, love, grief, healing, or courage.
I will remain in tune with the timing needed for myself and others.

Three things I will do when I need to slow down this week:

_____

_____

_____

_____

To what or whom will I give my time and attention?

_____

_____

_____

_____

I will show patience in these areas:

_____

_____

_____

_____

Intention:

_____

Affirmation:

_____

I am grateful for:

_____

_____

_____

_____

Personal Prayer/ Meditation/ Journal Entry:

_____

week three

forgiveness

I will search within for areas that need forgiveness.
I will lavish forgiveness on others who need it from me.

What areas in my life need forgiveness?

_____

_____

_____

_____

Someone I should share forgiveness with: _____

Why?_____

_____

_____

_____

Who has shown me grace? When?

_____

_____

_____

_____

Intention:

_____

Affirmation:

_____

I am grateful for:

_____

_____

_____

_____

Personal Prayer/ Meditation/ Journal Entry:

week four

confidence

Even in the uncertain seasons, I will hold my head up with confidence that I am right where I am meant to be. I am capable. I am worthy.

Favorite things about myself:

_____

_____

_____

_____

I know I am capable of...

_____

_____

_____

_____

I feel strongest when I...

_____

_____

_____

_____

Intention:

_____

Affirmation:

_____

I am grateful for:

_____

_____

_____

_____

Personal Prayer/ Meditation/ Journal Entry:

week five

listening to understand

I will listen with the intention to understand, not to respond.
I will give ear to my neighbor and if necessary, I will use my words.

I feel understood and important when someone…

_____

_____

_____

_____

Two people I will intentionally listen to this week:

_____

_____

_____

_____

(circle one) I normally…

do the talking   or   do the listening

listen to respond   or   listen to understand

Intention:

_____

Affirmation:

_____

I am grateful for:

_____

_____

_____

_____

Personal Prayer/ Meditation/ Journal Entry:

week six

the ebb and flow

On hard days I will be soft on myself.
On good days I will rejoice.
On both days I will be grateful.

To release the weight of a bad day, I will…

_____

_____

_____

_____

How can I celebrate the good in my days?

_____

_____

_____

_____

Two people I can count on to make me smile… Why?

_____

_____

_____

Intention:

_____

Affirmation:

_____

I am grateful for:

_____

_____

_____

_____

Personal Prayer/ Meditation/ Journal Entry:

week seven

keeping my commitments

...to myself and to those around me.
I will honor my words, striving to be dependable
to myself and to the needs of others.

What commitments have I made recently?

_____

_____

_____

_____

How will I hold myself accountable to my commitments?

_____

_____

_____

_____

When others depend on me, I feel...

_____

_____

_____

Intention:

_____

Affirmation:

_____

I am grateful for:

_____

_____

_____

_____

Personal Prayer/ Meditation/ Journal Entry:

week eight

rest

I will recognize when my mind and body need rest. I will shut out distractions that are unimportant in order to let rest take over.
Rest is important for healing and growing.

Besides sleeping, what are some ways to let my mind and body rest?

_____

_____

_____

_____

My body feels best when…

_____

_____

_____

_____

My mind is strongest when…

_____

_____

_____

Intention:

_____

Affirmation:

_____

I am grateful for:

_____

_____

_____

_____

Personal Prayer/ Meditation/ Journal Entry:

week nine

productivity

I will work at my craft, refine my skills, and sharpen my tools.
I will create goals and meet them without putting
unhealthy expectations on myself.

Personal goals for the week:

_____

_____

_____

_____

Career goals for the week:

_____

_____

_____

_____

Plan of attack:

_____

_____

_____

Intention:

_____

Affirmation:

_____

I am grateful for:

_____

_____

_____

_____

Personal Prayer/ Meditation/ Journal Entry:

week ten

feeling my feelings

Masking fear will not make me brave.
Hiding joy will not heal my grief.
Crying does not make me weak.
I will allow myself to feel.

What has brought me joy today?

_____

_____

_____

_____

What has been heavy on my heart?

_____

_____

_____

_____

Current fears:

_____

_____

_____

Intention:

_____

Affirmation:

_____

I am grateful for:

_____

_____

_____

_____

Personal Prayer/ Meditation/ Journal Entry:

week eleven

abandoning worry

The birds don't worry about food,
neither do the wildflowers worry about clothes.
I trust that I will have provision in the right timing. (Luke 12:22-31)

What worries have been on my heart and mind?

_____

_____

_____

_____

Three steps I'll take when worry starts to creep in:

_____

_____

_____

_____

Where can I go (physically or in my mind) to be at peace?

_____

_____

_____

Intention:

_____

Affirmation:

_____

I am grateful for:

_____

_____

_____

_____

Personal Prayer/ Meditation/ Journal Entry:

week twelve

thoughtful speech

I will listen to understand and respond with intention.
I will create authentic dialogue in my relationships
and speak kindly to myself and others.

A love letter to myself:

_____

_____

_____

_____

_____

What do I love about my best friend/significant other?

_____

_____

_____

_____

_____

…Now tell them! ☺

Intention:

_____

Affirmation:

_____

I am grateful for:

_____

_____

_____

_____

Personal Prayer/ Meditation/ Journal Entry:

week thirteen

love languages

I will practice speaking in love languages other than my own.
I will recognize when others receive love differently than me.
I will do my best to adjust the ways I show them love.

What is my love language and/or how do I feel most loved?

_____

_____

_____

_____

What are some ways I can show love to others this week?

_____

_____

_____

_____

I feel unloved when...

_____

_____

_____

Intention:

_____

Affirmation:

_____

I am grateful for:

_____

_____

_____

_____

Personal Prayer/ Meditation/ Journal Entry:

week fourteen

mindfulness

*I will practice being aware of my present moment,
acknowledging and accepting what I have around and before me,
showing gratitude for all of my blessings.*

Breathe in this moment. What do I hear, smell, feel, see, taste?

_____

_____

_____

_____

What do I notice first about my surrounding? (circle one)

Sight   Smell   Sound   Taste   Feel

A list of my blessings:

_____

_____

_____

_____

_____

_____

Intention:

_____

Affirmation:

_____

I am grateful for:

_____

_____

_____

_____

Personal Prayer/ Meditation/ Journal Entry:

week fifteen

listening to my body

I will recognize what brings me pain, anxiety, or anger.
I will proactively respond with intention instead of ignoring my body's needs.

What has my body been telling me lately? How can I better care for it?

_____

_____

_____

What will I do when my body is stressed or anxious?

_____

_____

_____

_____

This week I will plan a time to indulge in mind and body care.
This is what I will do:

Day:_____ Time:_____

_____

_____

_____

Intention:

_____

Affirmation:

_____

I am grateful for:

_____

_____

_____

_____

Personal Prayer/ Meditation/ Journal Entry:

week sixteen

serving others

I will share my blessings with the ones I love and the ones around me.
This will include my time, energy, and gifts.
When I care for myself, I am able to care for others.

Who will I intentionally serve this week? How?

_____

_____

_____

_____

When others serve and care for me, I feel...

_____

_____

_____

_____

How does serving others help me grow?

_____

_____

_____

Intention:

_____

Affirmation:

_____

I am grateful for:

_____

_____

_____

_____

Personal Prayer/ Meditation/ Journal Entry:

week seventeen

surrender

I will surrender what I cannot control,
what hurts my deepest parts,
and the wrongs I have done.
I will allow the weight to be lifted to experience grace.

The list of things out of my control that I will put down this week:

_____

_____

_____

_____

_____

When I am weighed down by life, I will take these steps to lighten my load:

_____

_____

_____

_____

_____

Intention:

_____

Affirmation:

_____

I am grateful for:

_____

_____

_____

_____

Personal Prayer/ Meditation/ Journal Entry:

week eighteen

positive presence

*I will recognize and remove myself from negative situations
so that I can be more available and present for the positive ones.*

What negative relationships or situations will I remove myself from?

_____

_____

_____

_____

For what situations will I show up fully and positively?

_____

_____

_____

_____

Showing up fully means…

_____

_____

_____

_____

Intention:

_____

Affirmation:

_____

I am grateful for:

_____

_____

_____

_____

Personal Prayer/ Meditation/ Journal Entry:

week nineteen

"maybe"

To prevent overcommitting and exhausting myself,
I will refrain from saying, "yes" to too many things.
However, I won't say, "no" before considering the possibilities in "maybe."

This week I will free up my schedule by...

_____

_____

_____

What do I look forward to accomplishing this week?
(goals, activities, the fun stuff too!)

_____

_____

_____

_____

My favorite way to wind down from the day:

_____

_____

_____

Intention:

_____

Affirmation:

_____

I am grateful for:

_____

_____

_____

_____

Personal Prayer/ Meditation/ Journal Entry:

week twenty

maximizing my gifts and talents

*I will utilize the gifts I have been given
to bless others and better myself.
I will practice my craft, knowing it can always improve.*

What talents do I possess?

_____

_____

_____

_____

How can I use these talents to serve my loved ones and my community?

_____

_____

_____

_____

How and when will I practice my craft this week?

_____

_____

_____

Intention:

_____

Affirmation:

_____

I am grateful for:

_____

_____

_____

_____

Personal Prayer/ Meditation/ Journal Entry:

week twenty-one

quality time

I will be intentional about the time I spend
with my loved ones and the time I spend alone.
I will do my best to be present mentally and emotionally — not just physically.

Who deserves my quality time?

_____

_____

_____

_____

What are some ways I will intentionally spend my time this week?

_____

_____

_____

_____

I will show up fully for _____ this week by...

_____

_____

_____

Intention:

_____

Affirmation:

_____

I am grateful for:

_____

_____

_____

_____

Personal Prayer/ Meditation/ Journal Entry:

week twenty-two

authenticity

*In a world where we are engrained, encouraged, and
pressured to put our "best self" on display at all times,
I will remain authentic in my words, my work, and my actions.
I will encourage others to do the same.*

What outside influences pressure me to "put on a front?"

_____

_____

_____

_____

Who do I feel most comfortable around? Why?

_____

_____

_____

_____

What can I offer others by sharing my authentic self?

_____

_____

_____

Intention:

_____

Affirmation:

_____

I am grateful for:

_____

_____

_____

_____

Personal Prayer/ Meditation/ Journal Entry:

week twenty-three

healthy boundaries

I will recognize unhealthy or toxic situations and relationships.
I will allow space when distance is necessary for growth.

Are there any relationships or situations I'm involved in that are
preventing healthy growth for me or my family?
(This could also be unhealthy uses of my time.)

_____

_____

_____

_____

Boundary Writing Practice
Set some healthy boundaries and make a plan to keep them:

_____

_____

_____

_____

_____

_____

_____

Intention:

_____

Affirmation:

_____

I am grateful for:

_____

_____

_____

_____

Personal Prayer/ Meditation/ Journal Entry:

week twenty-four

big and small victories

I will make the effort to recognize the accomplishments of myself and others.
I will boldly celebrate even the small victories.

What achievements – big or small - have I reached in the past weeks?

_____

_____

_____

_____

I challenge myself to celebrate my accomplishments by...

_____

_____

_____

_____

Who has experienced a victory recently? How can I celebrate them?

_____

_____

_____

_____

Intention:

_____

Affirmation:

_____

I am grateful for:

_____

_____

_____

_____

Personal Prayer/ Meditation/ Journal Entry:

week twenty-five

encouraging others

When someone cares, supports, and builds me up with their words,
I feel strong and important.
I will recognize opportunities to do the same for others.

Five encouraging affirmations I can share with any of my friends:

_____

_____

_____

_____

_____

Who do I know that could currently use some encouraging words?
Write them a letter here:

_____

_____

_____

_____

_____

_____

_____

Intention:

_____

Affirmation:

_____

I am grateful for:

_____

_____

_____

_____

Personal Prayer/ Meditation/ Journal Entry:

week twenty-six

discovering new joys

*I will search for the people, places, feelings, and
experiences that cause my heart to swell with gratitude.
I will recognize, rejoice, and return to them when I feel low.*

What brings me joy?

People: _____

Places: _____

Things: _____

Experiences: _____

Something new I have been wanting to try:

_____

_____

_____

If I could spend the day with any living person, who would it be? Why?

_____

_____

_____

_____

Intention:

_____

Affirmation:

_____

I am grateful for:

_____

_____

_____

_____

Personal Prayer/ Meditation/ Journal Entry:

week twenty-seven

standing in my truth

I will stand firm and grounded in my truth,
even if that means taking the road less traveled.
I will fiercely seek my purpose and live it out boldly.

What does it mean to me to stand firm in my truth?

_____

_____

_____

_____

What are some deep truths about how I live my life that may be unpopular to others?

_____

_____

_____

_____

What am I most proud of in my life?

_____

_____

_____

Intention:

_____

Affirmation:

_____

I am grateful for:

_____

_____

_____

_____

Personal Prayer/ Meditation/ Journal Entry:

week twenty-eight

tenderness

I will soften my heart to the feelings and needs of myself and others.
I will celebrate with the joyful, and grieve with the hurting.

When or with whom do I feel most tender?

_____

_____

_____

_____

Am I most often hard or soft on myself and others? Explain...

_____

_____

_____

_____

What makes me a good friend?

_____

_____

_____

_____

Intention:

_____

Affirmation:

_____

I am grateful for:

_____

_____

_____

_____

Personal Prayer/ Meditation/ Journal Entry:

week twenty-nine

carrying out responsibilities

*No matter how big or small of a task,
I will chip away at my goals and workload
so I can be fully present for the things that matter most to me.*

What responsibilities must I complete this week?

Home: _____

Work: _____

Personal: _____

Other: _____

How will I reward myself for completing my tasks?

_____

_____

_____

_____

What am I looking forward to this week?

_____

_____

_____

Intention:

_____

Affirmation:

_____

I am grateful for:

_____

_____

_____

_____

Personal Prayer/ Meditation/ Journal Entry:

week thirty

protecting my peace

I will not allow fear, worry, or doubt to occupy my mind or my time.
I will let go of these feelings. I will no longer allow them to rob me of my comfort and joy.

When doubt creeps in, I will…

_____

_____

_____

_____

Who can I run to when I am anxious or in fear?

_____

_____

_____

_____

Create a mantra for shifting moods when feeling low:

_____

_____

_____

Intention:

_____

Affirmation:

_____

I am grateful for:

_____

_____

_____

_____

Personal Prayer/ Meditation/ Journal Entry:

week thirty-one

vulnerability

I will allow others in. Asking for help does not make me weak.
Letting someone care for me will not stunt my growth.
It is a necessary part of self-care.

My favorite self-care activities include:

_____

_____

_____

_____

The next time I need help, I will...

_____

_____

_____

_____

Do I normally share my thoughts and feelings with others?
Why or why not?

_____

_____

_____

Intention:

_____

Affirmation:

_____

I am grateful for:

_____

_____

_____

_____

Personal Prayer/ Meditation/ Journal Entry:

week thirty-two

the pause

*When necessary, I will take a step away
to undress from life. I will be present for thought,
for prayer, for meditation, for discernment, and for quiet.*

What challenges in my life are weighing me down?

_____

_____

_____

_____

If I could go anywhere to experience the "pause," I would go to…

_____

_____

_____

_____

Ways I will unwind and pause this week:

_____

_____

_____

Intention:

_____

Affirmation:

_____

I am grateful for:

_____

_____

_____

_____

Personal Prayer/ Meditation/ Journal Entry:

week thirty-three

perserverance

*When I falter, fail, or something pushes me back, I will give myself grace.
I will dust off my hands and try again. I will do this over and over
until I accomplish what is needed for healthy growth.*

Three things I want to accomplish this week /month – big or small:

_____

_____

_____

_____

I am motivated by…

_____

_____

_____

Who are my biggest cheerleaders? Thank them here.
(Then share the words with them ☺)

_____

_____

_____

_____

Intention:

_____

Affirmation:

_____

I am grateful for:

_____

_____

_____

_____

Personal Prayer/ Meditation/ Journal Entry:

week thirty-four

the flow

I will be flexible and gentle to myself and others.
I will rewrite my story as many times as necessary.
I will be stretched, moved, and refined in order to grow.

How do I typically handle change?

_____

_____

_____

Write about a time when growth was uncomfortable.

_____

_____

_____

_____

Where do I see myself in five years?

_____

_____

_____

_____

Intention:

_____

Affirmation:

_____

I am grateful for:

_____

_____

_____

_____

Personal Prayer/ Meditation/ Journal Entry:

week thirty-five

self-care

I will take care of my whole self —
physically, mentally, emotionally, and spiritually.
I will identify and participate in activities that manage
my stress and support my wellbeing.

What is my current self-care routine? (Do I even have one?)

_____

_____

_____

_____

What makes me happy?

_____

_____

_____

What thought patterns are holding me back in my growth?

_____

_____

_____

_____

Intention:

_____

Affirmation:

_____

I am grateful for:

_____

_____

_____

_____

Personal Prayer/ Meditation/ Journal Entry:

week thirty-six

creativity

*I will participate in experiences that boost my creativity.
I will seek out opportunities to bring creativity into my daily life.*

A letter to my younger self:

_____

_____

_____

_____

_____

_____

Draw an encouraging banner:

Intention:

_____

Affirmation:

_____

I am grateful for:

_____

_____

_____

_____

Personal Prayer/ Meditation/ Journal Entry:

week thirty-seven

expectation

In seasons of waiting, I will wait with expectation that good will come.
I can find joy in the present because I expect that things will always get better.

Something I am waiting on:

_____

_____

_____

What is inspiring me right now?

_____

_____

_____

_____

My current priorities are…

_____

_____

_____

_____

Intention:

_____

Affirmation:

_____

I am grateful for:

_____

_____

_____

_____

Personal Prayer/ Meditation/ Journal Entry:

week thirty-eight

leadership

I will lead by example.
I will lead with humility.
I will lead with confidence.

Who was my favorite teacher? What qualities made him/her so great?

_____

_____

_____

Three things I am good at:

_____

_____

_____

_____

What I hope people will remember about me after I am gone...

_____

_____

_____

_____

Intention:

_____

Affirmation:

_____

I am grateful for:

_____

_____

_____

_____

Personal Prayer/ Meditation/ Journal Entry:

week thirty-nine

community

I will be involved in my community.
I will trust my community.
I will serve my community.

Who is my community? (family, friends, church, etc.)

_____

_____

_____

Am I active in my community? How so?

_____

_____

_____

How can I better serve my community?

_____

_____

_____

Intention:

_____

Affirmation:

_____

I am grateful for:

_____

_____

_____

_____

Personal Prayer/ Meditation/ Journal Entry:

week forty

physical health

My body is a temple. I will care for it by giving it proper nourishment and attention. I will choose a lifestyle that grows and grooms me in good health.

How do I feel physically?

_____

_____

_____

How do I want to feel?

_____

_____

_____

Five health goals for this month:

_____

_____

_____

_____

_____

Intention:

_____

Affirmation:

_____

I am grateful for:

_____

_____

_____

_____

Personal Prayer/ Meditation/ Journal Entry:

week forty-one

finances

*I have the responsibility and capability to make wise
decisions about my finances. I will be a good steward of money. I will
use it for the betterment of my life and the lives of others.*

Three short term financial goals:

_____

_____

_____

Three long term financial goals:

_____

_____

_____

_____

A plan for financial generosity:

_____

_____

_____

_____

Intention:

_____

Affirmation:

_____

I am grateful for:

_____

_____

_____

_____

Personal Prayer/ Meditation/ Journal Entry:

week forty-two

taking up space

I will not shrink myself to fit into spaces that are not made for me.
I will show up fully. I will take up space.
I will use my voice and share my truth.

I am proud of myself for…

_____

_____

_____

I will take up space this week by…

_____

_____

_____

_____

If I had no fear of failure, I would:

_____

_____

_____

_____

Intention:

_____

Affirmation:

_____

I am grateful for:

_____

_____

_____

_____

Personal Prayer/ Meditation/ Journal Entry:

week forty-three

inspiration

I will allow myself to draw inspiration from others without feeling guilty about my own life. I will celebrate and encourage the ones who inspire me.

Who inspires me the most? Why?

_____

_____

_____

_____

What am I really good at?

_____

_____

_____

_____

What traits do I admire in others?

_____

_____

_____

Intention:

_____

Affirmation:

_____

I am grateful for:

_____

_____

_____

_____

Personal Prayer/ Meditation/ Journal Entry:

week forty-four

vision

I will allow myself to dream and create visions for the future.
I will put in the time and effort to manifest these dreams into reality.

What did my life look like five years ago?

_____

_____

_____

_____

_____

My ten year vision:

_____

_____

_____

_____

_____

_____

_____

Intention:

_____

Affirmation:

_____

I am grateful for:

_____

_____

_____

_____

Personal Prayer/ Meditation/ Journal Entry:

week forty-five

faith

I will boldly live out my faith and truth.
I will be involved in my faith community.
I will use my time and my resources to be more engaged.
I will sink my roots deeper into the truths
that have been planted in my heart.

How is my spiritual life? What areas need maturing?

_____

_____

_____

_____

Who has been an inspiration to me in my walk of faith? Why?

_____

_____

_____

How will I spend more time watering and nurturing my faith?

_____

_____

_____

Intention:

_____

Affirmation:

_____

I am grateful for:

_____

_____

_____

_____

Personal Prayer/ Meditation/ Journal Entry:

week forty-six

enough

I affirm that I am enough. I affirm that I have enough.
I will be content with all that I am and all that I have.

Material things I possess that I can do without:

_____

_____

_____

Thoughts, ideals, and circumstances I want less of in my life:

_____

_____

_____

_____

If I had to move away with nothing except five items, I would take…

_____

_____

_____

_____

Intention:

_____

Affirmation:

_____

I am grateful for:

_____

_____

_____

_____

Personal Prayer/ Meditation/ Journal Entry:

week forty-seven

home

Where I find rest, and love, and truth, and sanctuary… that is home.
I will remember to come home.

In my home, my favorite place is… Why?

_____

_____

_____

Where is "home" for me? Who is there?

_____

_____

_____

_____

Do I truly feel "at home" currently in my life? Why or why not?

_____

_____

_____

_____

Intention:

_____

Affirmation:

_____

I am grateful for:

_____

_____

_____

_____

Personal Prayer/ Meditation/ Journal Entry:

week forty-eight

impact

I will not shrink myself by doing nothing for others. I have the ability to impact one person and I have the ability to impact the world.

How can I impact the world with my abilities?

_____

_____

_____

Who is one person I have heavily impacted this year? How?

_____

_____

_____

_____

If money was not an issue, what would I do to make a difference in my community?

_____

_____

_____

_____

Intention:

_____

Affirmation:

_____

I am grateful for:

_____

_____

_____

_____

Personal Prayer/ Meditation/ Journal Entry:

week forty-nine

addressing my guilt or shame

I will do the inner work to address the areas of my life that I have not forgiven. My past does not define me. I am capable of living an abundant life.

What am I afraid to tell others about myself or my past?

_____

_____

_____

_____

What do I need to forgive myself for?

_____

_____

_____

I believe I will live abundantly because…

_____

_____

_____

_____

Intention:

_____

Affirmation:

_____

I am grateful for:

_____

_____

_____

Personal Prayer/ Meditation/ Journal Entry:

week fifty

love

I will love with intention. I will search for love with intention.
I will guard my heart above all things.

What qualities are important to me in a significant other?

_____

_____

_____

What is the kindest gesture someone has done to show me love?

_____

_____

_____

_____

What scares me about love?

_____

_____

_____

_____

Intention:

_____

Affirmation:

_____

I am grateful for:

_____

_____

_____

_____

Personal Prayer/ Meditation/ Journal Entry:

week fifty-one

career success

I will set high, realistic, and healthy expectations for myself in my career.
I will hold myself accountable for my successes and shortcomings.

How do I balance work and life?

_____

_____

_____

What are my current career goals?

_____

_____

_____

_____

What does success in my career look like to me?

_____

_____

_____

_____

Intention:

_____

Affirmation:

_____

I am grateful for:

_____

_____

_____

_____

Personal Prayer/ Meditation/ Journal Entry:

week fifty-two

tending to my needs

*I will water myself first, so that I remain capable of
pouring into those around me. I cannot give if I am empty.*

What is something I have been needing (or wanting) to do for myself
that I have been putting off?

_____

_____

_____

_____

One thing I will do for myself before I go to bed each night this week:

_____

_____

My self-care intentions for the New Year:

_____

_____

_____

_____

_____

Intention:

_____

Affirmation:

_____

I am grateful for:

_____

_____

_____

_____

Personal Prayer/ Meditation/ Journal Entry:

Connect further with Ka'ala

Instagram: @alohakaala
Website: www.alohakaala.com

Made in USA - Crawfordsville, IN
58407_9781708555719
10.11.2021 1825